P9-CDT-611

NATIONAL GEOGRAPHIC KiDS

AMAZING ANIMALS
SUPER STICKER ACTIVITY BOOK
★ TWO BOOKS IN ONE!

Inside this book:

Cool Animals

Dinos

Pull out the sticker sheets and keep them by you as you complete each page. There are also lots of extra stickers to use in the book or anywhere you want! Have fun!

NATIONAL GEOGRAPHIC
Washington, D.C.

Editorial, Design, and Production by
make believe ideas

Picture credits: pp1–40: all images Shutterstock except for: Fotolia: 18 tm, 29 m; Fotosearch: 38 bl; Make Believe Ideas: 1 tl, 2 tl; bl, 3 tl, 4 mr; br, 5 br, 9 tl; m; bm, 11 br, 12 ml,13 tm, 14 ml, 16 ml; mr, 17 br (olive leaf), 18 tl; br; bm, 21 mr (yellow/black frog), 22 mr, 23 tr; m; br; bm, 25 bl, 26 tl; tm; tr, 28 m, 30 bm; br, 32 mr; m; br, 33 tr; bm (beetle x2),35 bl, 36 bl; bm; br, 37 br, 40 mr; bl; Mark O'Shea: 15 ml (gecko); National Geographic Stock: 2 8 br, 21 tr (American green tree frog), 24 tr, 33 mr, 36 ml, 40 tm. Sticker pages: all images Shutterstock except for: Fotolia: 28,29 silver fish bl; Fotosearch: 4,5 purple jellyfish; turtle, 10,11 purple jellyfish, 38,39 stingray; purple jellyfish; Make Believe Ideas: 2,3 frog; olive leaf; tortoise; yellow butterfly; parrot; daisy; tiger face; owl; blue butterfly, 4,5 one spot foxface; golden butterfly fish; starfish; black/yellow fish small; queen angelfish; spiral shell; green fish; whelk shell; cockleshell, 6,7 sweets; football; cupcake, 8,9 zebra x2; mountain goat; butterfly x3; tortoise; lizard; tiger x2; lion x3; California kingsnake; rhino x2; giraffe x3; elephant; crocodile, 10,11 seahorse; cinnamon anemonefish; one spot foxface; blacktip reef shark; cockleshell; green fish;black/yellow fish small; golden butterfly fish; queen angelfish; whelk shell; starfish, 12,13 seagull, 14,15 spider m; beetles tl, m, bl, br, mr, tr; leaf insect x2; olive leaf, 16,17 spiders ml, bm, tr; fly bl, mr, 20,21 frogs tl, tm, tr, bm, 22,23 baboon and young; train; ice cream; donut; dusky leaf monkey; sunglasses; monkey toy; car; gibbon; spoon; toothbrush, 24,25 lion x2; tiger x3; black leopard br; jaguar, 28,29 green fish; sardine, 30,31 giraffe tm, tr, m; flamingo,32,33 spade; marbles; snake; burrowing scorpion; hat, 34,35 sandwich; gingerbread; boat; rose; watch; scissors, 36,37 polar bear x2; snowy owl; sealions; fur seal; reindeer, 38,39 cockleshell; crab; starfish; one spot foxface; golden butterfly fish; yellow/black fish small; seahorse; whelk shell; spiral shell; queen angelfish; green fish, 40 parrot; bat; red-eyed tree frog x2; tiger x2; milksnake; red leaf x3; rockhopper penguin; rabbit x2; zebra; mountain goat; olive leaf; lion x2; northern saw-whet owl; elephant; rhino x2; emerald tree boa; hamadryas baboon; California kingsnake; giraffe x2; iguana; kitten; polar bear; beetles tl, tm, tr, ml, m, mr, bl, br; stag beetle x2; leaf insect; tarantula; moth; cockroach; Mark O'Shea: 14,15 tm (gecko); National Geographic Stock: 22,23 golden marmoset x2, 32,33 meerkat, 40 otter; 123RF: 10,11 desjardini tang, 36,37 yellow tang, 38,39 Hawaiian squirrelfish; desjardini tang.

Printed in China. 20/MBI/6

Turn the page for *Cool Animals!*

Every tiger has a different pattern of stripes!

Color a tiger pattern!

Color and sticker more amazing animals with spots and stripes!

Sticker a hunting tiger!

What animal is this?
Complete the word.

zebra

Sharks are amazing!

Sticker a blacktip reef shark!

lemon shark

zebra shark

clownfish

WARNING

Use the grid to draw a shark!

Draw here

4

Sticker a shark's tooth!

Sticker a hammerhead shark!

great white shark

Sharks have sharp teeth and powerful bodies.

Color the sea life and sticker more fish friends!

What else lives in the ocean?

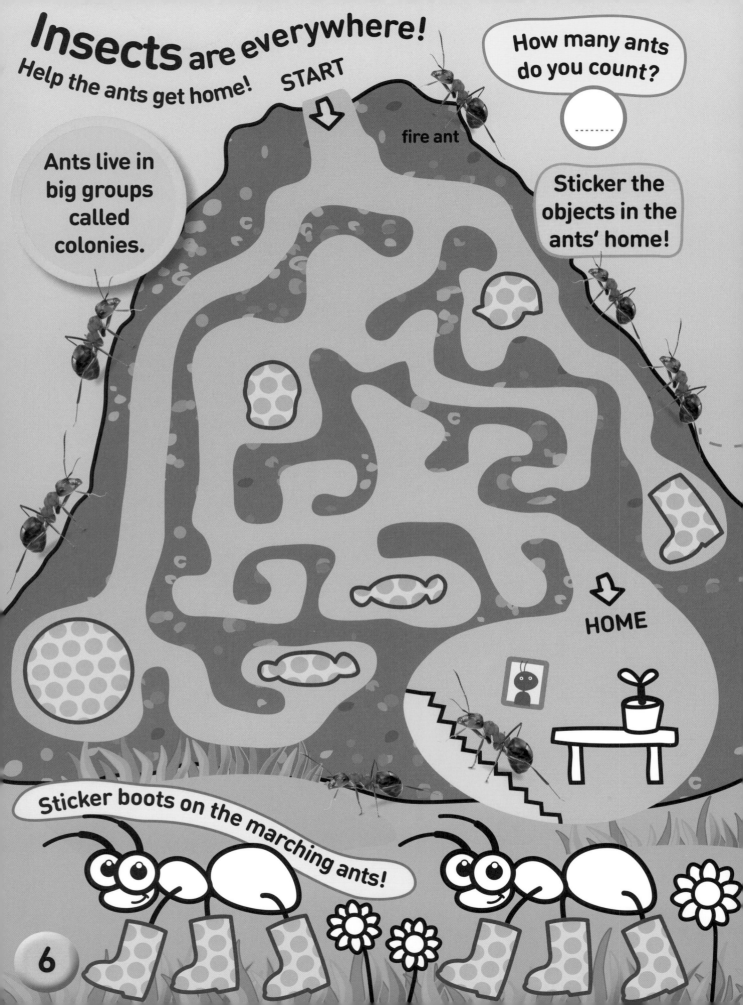

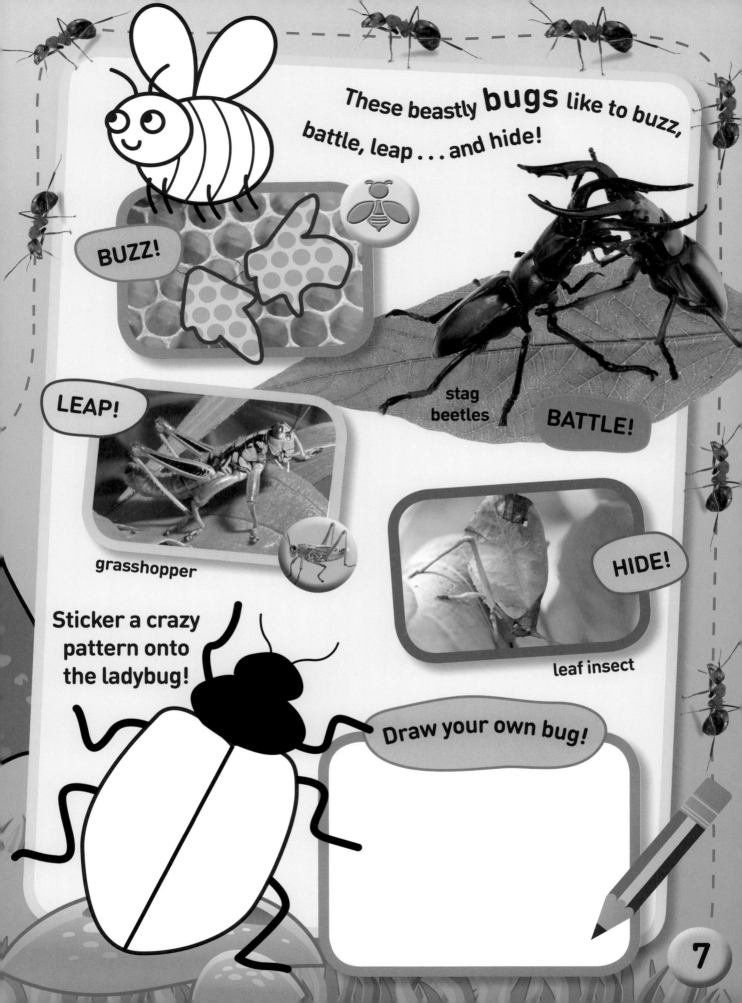

These beastly **bugs** like to buzz, battle, leap . . . and hide!

BUZZ!

stag beetles

BATTLE!

LEAP!

grasshopper

HIDE!

leaf insect

Sticker a crazy pattern onto the ladybug!

Draw your own bug!

7

Elephants are **big** and **strong**.

Find your way through the elephant maze.

START ⇩

FINISH ⇩

OUCH! Let go!

Draw the other half of the elephant.

Elephants are the largest animals that live on land today.

8

Sticker animals at the water hole.

African elephants

hippo

Sticker this dangerous animal!

bongo

impala

What lives under the sea?

Finish the dot-to-dot, then add color!

5
6
7
4
1
11
12
3
13
10
8
2
9
14
15
18
17
16

Octopuses do not have skeletons!

hawksbill
sea turtle

Color the animals and add stickers to complete the ocean scene.

10

Scary fish

Draw more teeth!

Ugly

wolffish

Scary and hairy

striated frogfish

anglerfish

blacktip reef shark

reef
squid

11

black-headed gull

START

HOME

guillemots

kittiwakes

Many seabirds nest on cliffs in big groups called colonies.

Sticker the missing feet on the blue-footed boobies!

13

Who's watching?

Lizards love to eat **bugs.**

YUM YUM

veiled chameleon

Madagascar day gecko

Draw the lizards' tongues.

leopard gecko

Sticker the yummy bugs!

green iguana

14

panther chameleon

panther chameleon

juvenile veiled chameleon

Sticker more leaves.

A gecko in danger can detach its tail to distract a predator and escape.

frilled lizard

tokay gecko

Some lizards have frills.

Some lizards have horns.

Sticker the missing horn, tail, and frill.

Jackson's chameleon

frilled lizard

Spiders have long legs!

Finish a spidery dot-to-dot, then add color.

Sticker spiders that are hanging around!

4●

3● ●5

2● ●6

20●   ●22   1●
    ●16   ●21   7●
  ●15   8●
  ●14   ●9
13●
19● ●17
12●   ●10
18●
11   Who lives in the leaves?

16

Tarantulas live under the ground instead of making webs.

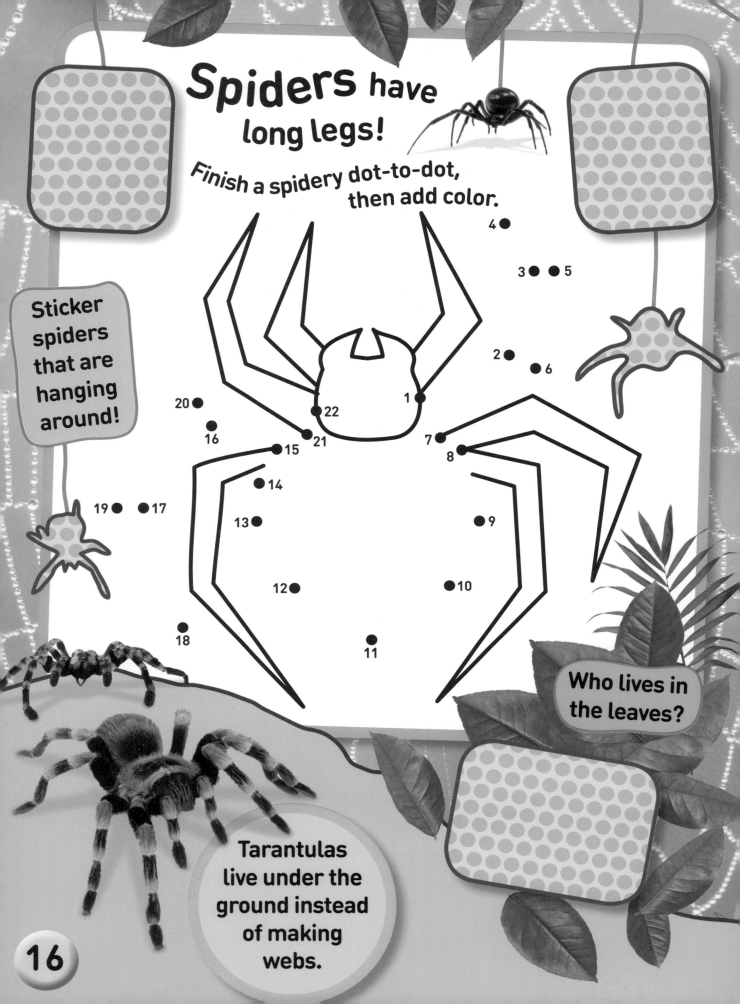

Sticker flies for the spiders to eat.

Some spiders spin webs to catch food.

orb weaver

giant orb weaver

Most spiders have eight eyes.

jumping spider

Find who is hiding in the pots!

black widow

Wolves are great hunters!

Follow the lines to see who found the deer!

gray wolves

Sticker more wolf tracks!

Sticker the wolves coming out to play!

fallow deer

Use the grid to draw a wolf!

Draw here

Finish the dot-to-dot, then add color!

1
2
3
20
21
4
19
5
8
13
14
6
7
12
18
9
11
15
17
10
16

Wolves can find each other across long distances by howling.

Wolves live in groups called packs.

gray wolves

Sticker the missing howling wolves!

Frogs can have amazing colors and patterns.

red-eyed tree frog

red-backed poison frog

white-lipped tree frog

Find the colorful frog stickers, then color the lily pads to match the frogs!

20

Sticker jumping frogs.

Some frogs can jump over 50 times their own body length!

African bullfrog

blue poison dart frog

black-and-yellow poison dart frog

American green tree frog

strawberry poison dart frog

How many frogs landed on the leaf?

Sticker spots onto the frog and add color.

Who's climbing?

21

It's a **primate** party!

scarlet macaw

What has the baboon stolen?

Most monkeys and apes like to sleep in a cozy nest built out of branches.

hamadryas baboon

Color this happy monkey!

CUTE!

SCARY!

Sticker more primates!

Sticker some banana snacks for the gorilla.

silverback gorilla

Draw a monkey face!

chimpanzee

23

Africa is home to cool cats!

What does the lion say?

A lioness has no mane and looks after cubs.

Sticker lion cubs!

Color the lion!

Draw and color tall grass to hide the lion!

24

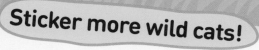

blue-and-yellow macaw

Sticker more wild cats!

cheetah

Burmese python

California kingsnake

milksnake

Snakes that hiss and rattle!

Snakes, like all reptiles, shed their skin to reveal a new layer.

royal python

Sticker a bright pattern onto the snake!

Find 5 snake eggs hidden on the page!

Who's hiding?

green tree python

Color the snakes and find the one that's different!

emerald tree boa

START

Wiggle your way through the snake maze!

Color the cobra!

king cobra

FINISH

27

Creatures with paws and claws!

What do bears shout?

Bears have big paws.

grizzly bear paw

Bears can catch fish as they swim upstream!

Sticker fish in the stream!

brown bear

28

Koalas aren't bears. They are actually related to kangaroos!

SLEEPING!

Sticker who is hiding in the eucalyptus leaves!

EATING!

CLIMBING!

START

FINISH

Help Mom find her baby!

Color the climbing koalas!

29

Giraffes are really tall!

Sticker the missing giraffes.

Sticker a pattern and color the giraffe.

Giraffes have very long gray tongues!

30

Draw, color, and sticker to make fun animal faces!

Add the stickers, then follow the lines to see who gets to the water.

31

Desert creatures
beat the heat!

How many beetles do you see?
....

A scorpion has a stinger in its tail.

Taurus beetle

imperial scorpion

Sticker more scorpions!

rhinoceros beetle

Color the beetle!

ground beetle

burrowing scorpion

white-spotted assassin bug

figeater beetle

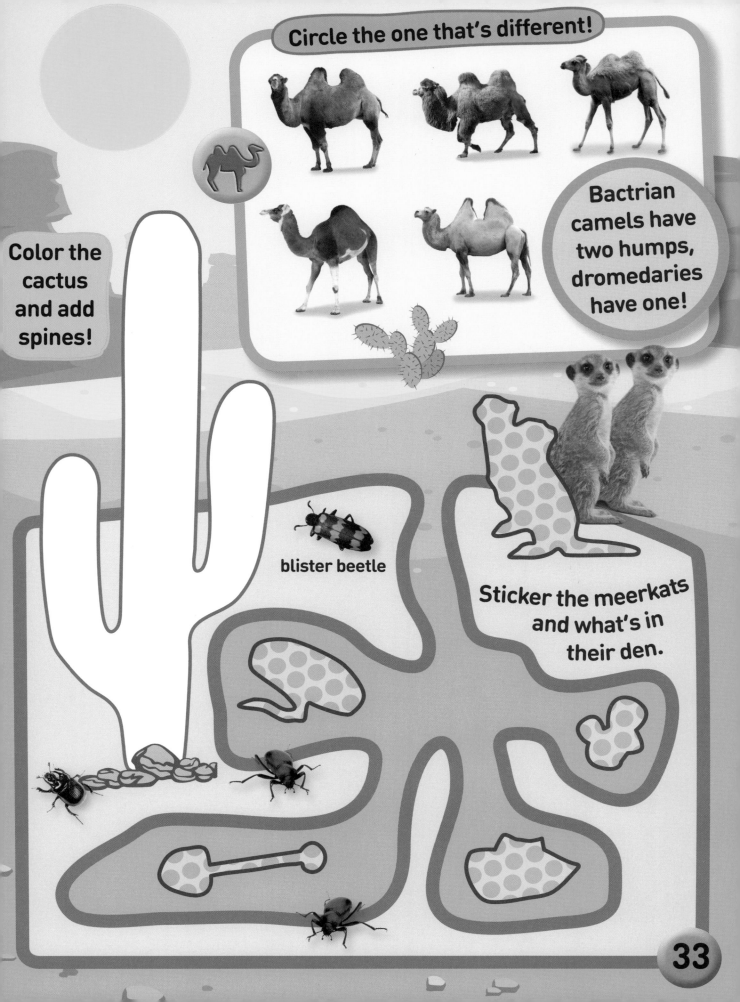

Circle the one that's different!

Color the cactus and add spines!

Bactrian camels have two humps, dromedaries have one!

blister beetle

Sticker the meerkats and what's in their den.

33

Birds clean their feathers daily. This is called preening.

Chatty birds fly high!

Sticker the flying macaws!

rainbow lorikeets

Sticker a colorful song!

What has the cockatoo stolen for his nest?

scarlet macaw

Color the parrot's tail.

sulphur-crested cockatoo

Sticker some eggs!

Help the toucan find his way home!

START

Toucans and cockatoos nest in holes in trees.

HOME

Toucans' beaks are actually made of very light bone!

Color the keel-billed toucan's beak!

Guianan toucanet

35

Animals have icy adventures!

Find a snowy owl!

Sticker more animals who live in the snow!

Arctic fox

Arctic hare

Sticker animals playing by the icy water!

rockhopper penguin

fur seal

Adélie penguin

Penguins cannot fly, but they swim very well!

Use the grid to finish drawing the penguin!

Follow the lines to see which penguin gets to the water!

king penguin

Sticker more snowflakes!

Color the penguin's bucket, then fill it with fish!

Adélie penguin

37

loggerhead
sea turtle

Turtles and rays
are awesome!

Sea turtles
can live up to
80 years!

Sticker the
missing sea
creatures!

Color the ray and
draw more spots!

blue-spotted
stingray

Sticker and color animals hiding in the seaweed!

Circle the fish that is different!

bannerfish

copperband butterfly fish

blue ring angelfish

clownfish

yellow boxfish

multibarred angelfish

39

Awesome animals!

red-eyed tree frog

bottlenose dolphins

rainbow finch

orangutan

green iguana

Who is stealing the eggs?

A polar bear has black skin!

polar bear

Sticker the animals eating!

Who is upside down?

Sticker and draw your favorite animals!

40

Stickers for pages 2 and 3

Stickers for pages 4 and 5

Stickers for pages 6 and 7

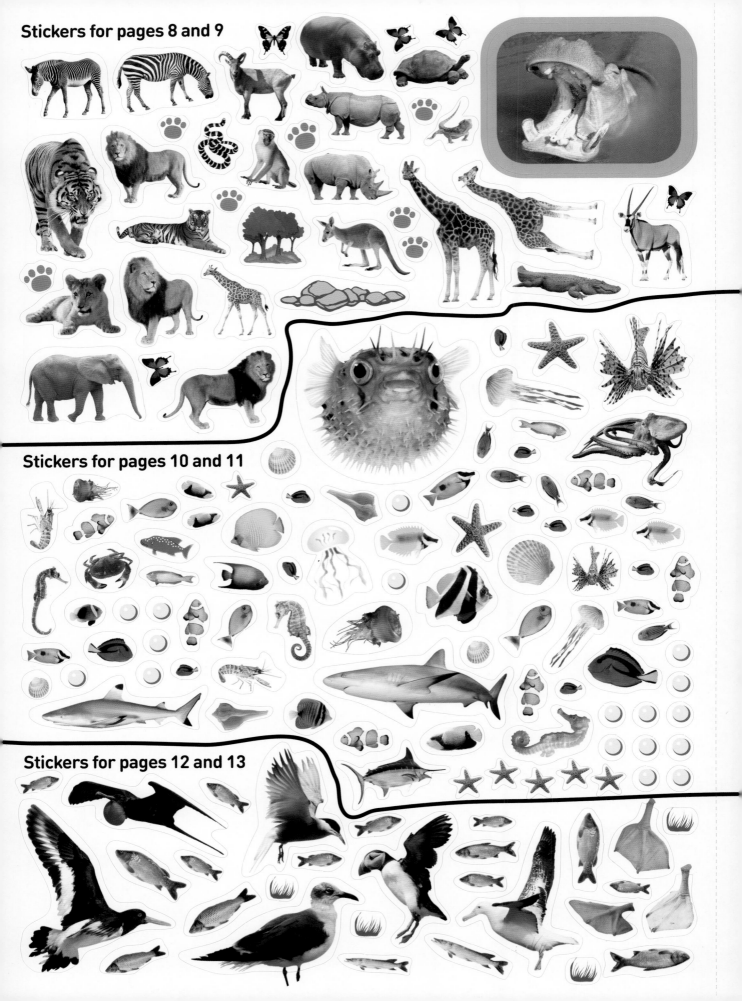

Stickers for pages 8 and 9

Stickers for pages 10 and 11

Stickers for pages 12 and 13

Stickers for pages 14 and 15

Stickers for pages 16 and 17

Stickers for pages 18 and 19

Stickers for pages 20 and 21

Stickers for pages 22 and 23

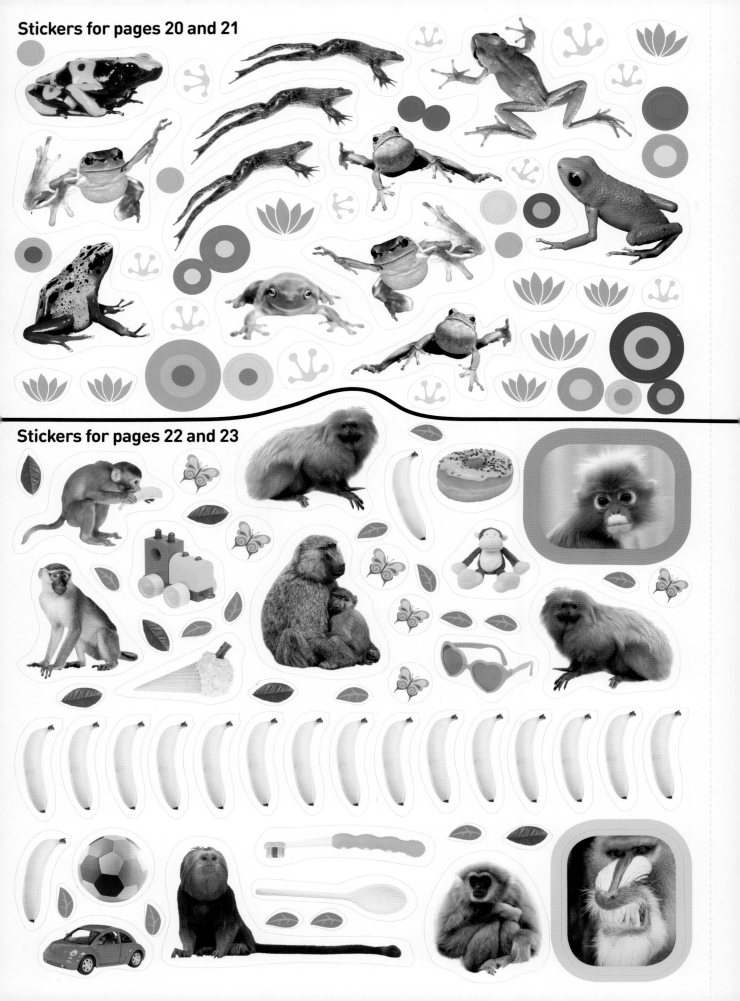

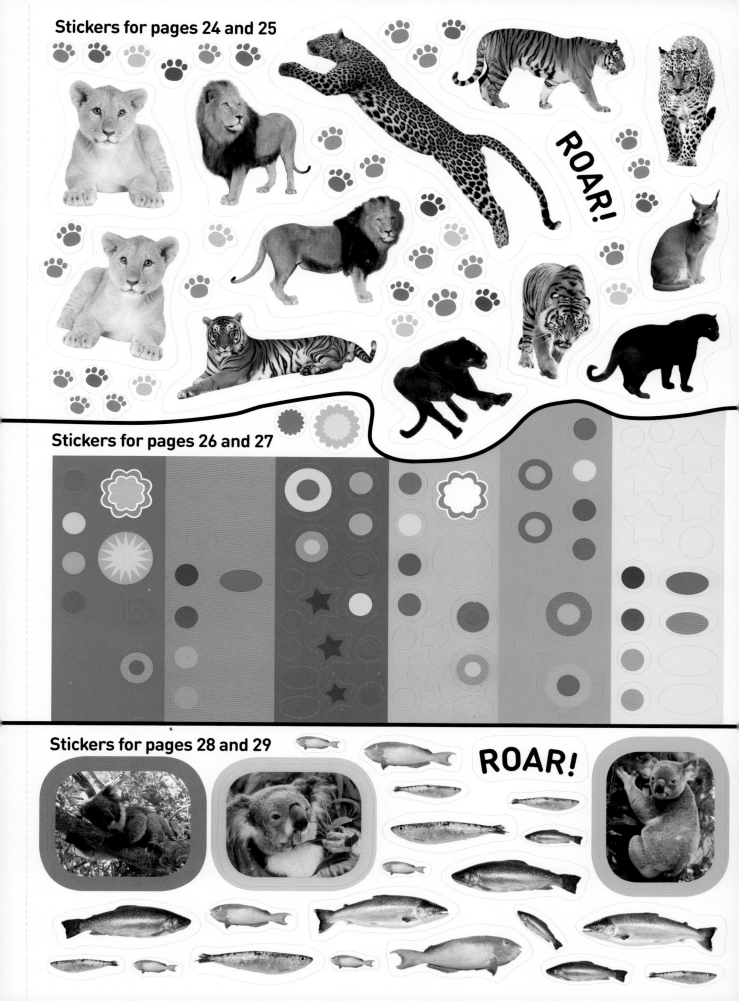

Stickers for pages 24 and 25

ROAR!

Stickers for pages 26 and 27

Stickers for pages 28 and 29

ROAR!

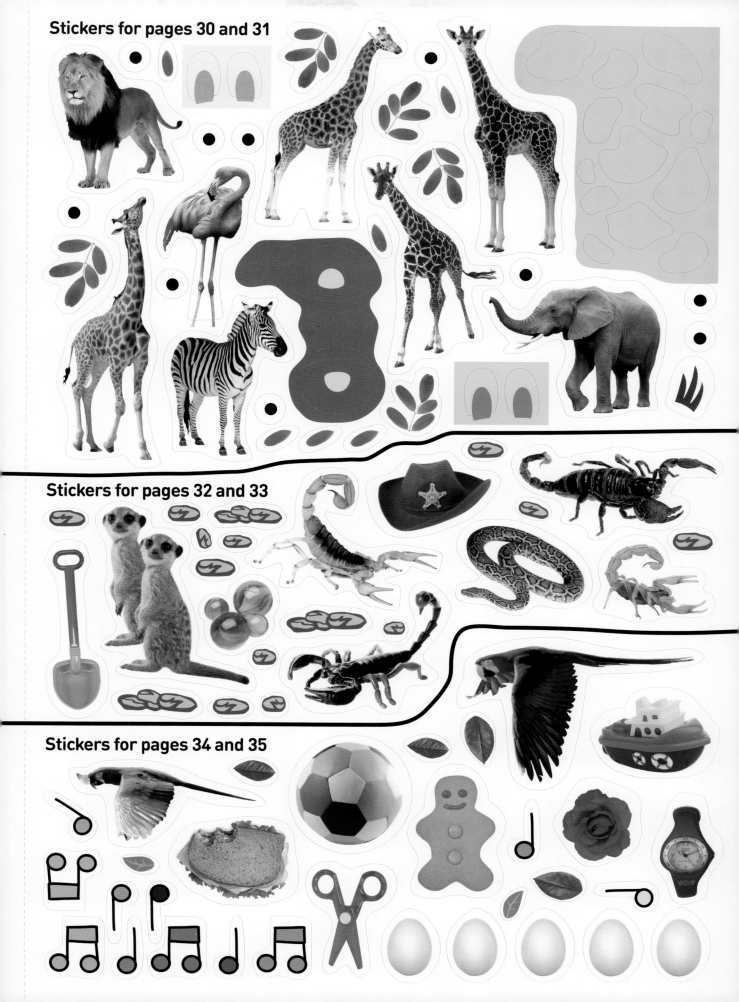

Stickers for pages 30 and 31

Stickers for pages 32 and 33

Stickers for pages 34 and 35

Stickers for pages 36 and 37

HOOT!

Stickers for pages 38 and 39

Stickers for page 40

Extra stickers

NATIONAL GEOGRAPHIC KIDS

AMAZING ANIMALS
SUPER STICKER ACTIVITY BOOK
☟ TWO BOOKS IN ONE!

Inside this book:

Cool Animals

Dinos

Pull out the sticker sheets and keep
them by you as you complete each page.
There are also lots of extra stickers to use
in the book or anywhere you want!
Have fun!

NATIONAL GEOGRAPHIC
Washington, D.C.

Editorial, Design, and Production by
make believe ideas

Consultant: Peter Ricketts Picture credits: All dinosaur artwork by Franco Tempesta/National Geographic unless as follows: DAMN FX/National Geographic Creative: 35 tl; John Sibbick/National Geographic Creative: 36 tm (Pteranodon); Make Believe Ideas: 1 tl; ml; mr, 2 tr, 2, 3 m (T. rex), 3 tl; ml; m; mr, 4 tm; mr; br, 5 br (branch), 6, 7 m (Diplodocus), 7 bl, 9 ml, 12 tr, 14 tl; mr, 15 tl; ml; mr; bl, 19 m, 20 mr, 24 ml; mr; bm; br, 25 tl; ml; br, 26 ml; mr; maze images: Allosaurus x2: tr; m, 27 tr; m, 29 tm; mr, 30 tl; bl; br, 31 mr (Parasaurolophus x3); bl, 33 mr (dragonfly); mr (butterfly), 34 tl, 34, 35 m (Kronosaurus), 36 tm; m (pterosaur x2); mr; bl (pterosaur x2); br, 36, 37 (background), 37 tm; mr; bm (pterosaur x3); bl (pterosaur); bl (ball); br (red pterosaur); br (seaweed); Make Believe Ideas/Graham Kennedy: 30 tm; ml; mr; Shutterstock: 3 bm (leaves x6); bm (eggs x2), 6 m, 8 tr (background), 14 ml; bm (background); 15 bm, 17 mr, 21 tm; tr, 24, 25 b (background), 26 maze images: Ceratosaurus x2: mr; bl, leaf: br, 33 mr (seeds), 36 bm; Xing Lida/National Geographic Creative: 33 bm. Sticker pages: All dinosaur artwork by Franco Tempesta/National Geographic unless as follows: John Sibbick/National Geographic Creative: 12, 13 Oviraptor, 36, 37 Quetzalcoatlus, 40 Alamosaurus; Anchiceratops; Dromiceiomimus; Troodon; Make Believe Ideas: 2, 3 Pteranodon x2; T. rex x4, 4, 5 bones x2; leaves x3 (combined); dinosaurs x4; birds x4, 6, 7 dinosaurs x7, 8, 9 Amargasaurus; Iguanodon, 10, 11 Pachycephalosaurus; Dilophosaurus, 14, 15 dinosaurs x3; dinosaur skulls x2; teddy bear, 20, 21 Deinonychus, 22, 23 Ankylosaurus, 24, 25 horns x3; Triceratops skull (medium), 26, 27 Ankylosaurus x2; tangerine, 28, 29 4x4; school bus; igloo; bed; Apatosaurus, 32, 33 ice cream; T-shirt, 36, 37 pterosaur; Pteranodon, 38, 39 skulls x2; skeleton; Make Believe Ideas/Graham Kennedy: 30, 31 Corythosaurus (matching activity); Saurolophus; Lambeosaurus; Pixeldust Studios/National Geographic Creative: 10, 11 Carnotaurus, 16, 17 Masiakasaurus; Raul Martin/National Geographic Creative: 34, 35 Deinosuchus; Shutterstock: 2, 3 eggs x3, 4, 5 leaf x4, 24, 25 Triceratops skull (small) x2, 28, 29 boat; house; Argentinosaurus, 34, 35 Plesiosaurus; Xing Lida/National Geographic Creative: 32, 33 Caudipteryx; Microraptor x4. Make Believe Ideas dinosaur images from products supplied by: www.dinosaurtime.co.uk.

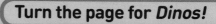

Turn the page for *Dinos!*

What is a **dinosaur?**

Dinosaurs were animals that lived more than 65 million years ago.

Color T. rex's scaly skin!

Tyrannosaurus rex
tye-RAN-oh-SORE-us rex

Find the missing stickers to finish T. rex!

scaly skin

long tail

2

Pteranodon
teh-RAN-uh-don

Dinosaurs lived on land. Animals that flew or lived in the ocean are not called dinosaurs.

sharp teeth

Elasmosaurus
el-LAZ-moe-SORE-us

Dinosaurs hatched from eggs. Sticker more eggs!

claws

3

Meet the different dinos!

Dinosaurs were either lizard-hipped like Allosaurus or bird-hipped like Stegosaurus.

Allosaurus
AL-oh-SORE-us

Sticker the different hip bones onto the skeletons.

Stegosaurus
STEG-oh-SORE-us

Bird-hipped dinosaurs ate only plants.

Sticker tasty plants for the dinosaur to eat.

Parasaurolophus
pa-ra-SORE-OH-lo-fus

BIRD-HIPPED

Triceratops
tri-SERR-ah-tops

Stegosaurus

Sticker the dinos to discover which group they belonged to.

LIZARD-HIPPED

T. rex

Brachiosaurus
BRACK-ee-oh-SORE-us

Some lizard-hipped dinosaurs are the ancestors of today's birds!

Color the dinosaur.

Sticker the birds!

Velociraptor *vel-OSS-ee-rap-tor*

5

The age of the dinosaurs

Help the dino get through the maze to his friend!

Start

Finish

Dinosaurs lived through different time periods called the Triassic, Jurassic, and Cretaceous.

Sticker the dinosaurs on the time line to see when they lived!

Plateosaurus
PLAT-ee-oh-SORE-us

Coelophysis
seel-OH-fie-sis

Diplodocus
dih-PLOD-uh-kus

Stegosaurus

6

252 million years ago
Triassic

201 million years ago
Jurassic

Use the grid to draw the dino!

Eoraptor   *EE-oh-RAP-tor*

Eoraptor was one of the earliest dinosaurs we know about.

Parasaurolophus

Triceratops

Ankylosaurus
AN-kee-lo-SORE-us

Deinonychus
die-NON-i-kus

Spinosaurus
SPINE-oh-SORE-us

Allosaurus

**145 million years ago
Cretaceous**

7

Cool Triassic, Jurassic, and Cretaceous dinos

TRIASSIC

Coelophysis was a carnivore, which means it ate other animals.

Coelophysis

Herrerasaurus
huh-RARE-ah-SORE-us

Riojasaurus
REE-oh-hah-SORE-us

Help Coelophysis find its food!

8

Finish the erupting volcano!

JURASSIC

Scientists used Archaeopteryx's fossils to discover that birds are related to dinosaurs.

Archaeopteryx
ARK-ee-OP-turr-icks

Yangchuanosaurus
YANG-chew-an-oh-SORE-us

Sticker colorful dino feathers!

Brachiosaurus

CRETACEOUS

These Cretaceous dinosaurs were . . .

TINY!

Microraptor
MY-cro-RAP-tore

SPIKY!

Find the missing stickers.

SPINY!

Amargasaurus
uh-MARG-uh-SORE-us

FIERCE!

T. rex

FRILLY!

Iguanodon
ig-WAN-oh-don

Triceratops

9

Weird and wonderful dinos

Find the missing stickers and color the picture frames!

Although Therizinosaurus's claws were about 28 inches (70 cm) long, it probably ate only plants!

Therizinosaurus
THERE-ih-ZIN-oh-SORE-us

Carnotaurus
KAR-no-TORE-us

Pachycephalosaurus had an ultra-thick skull!

Carnotaurus had really tiny arms!

Pachycephalosaurus
pack-ee-SEF-ah-lo-SORE-us

Draw a funny dinosaur face!

Ouranosaurus had super spines!

Ouranosaurus
oo-RAHN-oh-SORE-us

Shunosaurus
SHOO-noh-SORE-us

Shunosaurus had a cool club-tail!

Dilophosaurus
die-LOAF-oh-sore-us

Dilophosaurus had a crest on its head.

Design your own cool crest using color and stickers!

11

Baby dinos hatched from eggs!

Dinosaurs laid hard-shelled eggs, just like birds. Many dinosaurs probably had feathers, too!

Color and sticker the eggs, then circle the one that's cracked!

Oviraptor
OH-vih-RAP-tore

Oviraptors built nests for their young.

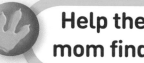

Help the dinosaur mom find her baby!

Maiasaura
MA-ya-SORE-a

Predators hunted other animals for food.

Help Allosaurus find its meal!

Allosaurus

Allosaurus was a meat-eater. Its sharp teeth were up to 4 inches (10 cm) long!

Stegosaurus

Sticker these predators' skulls!

Allosaurus

Ceratosaurus
seh-RAT-oh-sore-us

Rajasaurus
RAH-jah-SORE-us

predator

T. rex

prey

fish

prey

Triceratops

predator

Spinosaurus

Predators are animals that chase and kill other animals. The animals they kill are their prey.

The tiny meat-eater Compsognathus was only as big as a turkey!

Compsognathus
KOMP-sog-NAH-thus

Color Compsognathus hiding in the bushes.

Deinonychus

Sticker more meat-eaters!

Tenontosaurus
ten-ON-toe-SORE-us

15

T. rex's arms weren't long enough to reach its mouth!

Give the dinosaur amazing arms, then decorate it with stickers and color.

T. rex

Giganotosaurus
gig-an-OH-toe-SORE-us

Masiakasaurus
mash-YUCK-uh-SORE-us

17

Spinosaurus and Baryonyx
were fierce fish-eaters!

Spinosaurus and Baryonyx had sharp teeth and hook-like claws to grab fish!

Baryonyx
bah-ree-ON-icks

Spinosaurus

Find out who will reach the fishy dinner!

18

Spinosaurus could grow to about 50 feet (15.2 m) long, and its spines were at least 5 feet (1.5 m) tall!

Color the amazing spines!

Sticker and color more fish for Spinosaurus.

Velociraptor and Deinonychus
were speedy predators!

Help Deinonychus find its prey.

Deinonychus

Parasaurolophus

Connect the dots to discover Deinonychus!

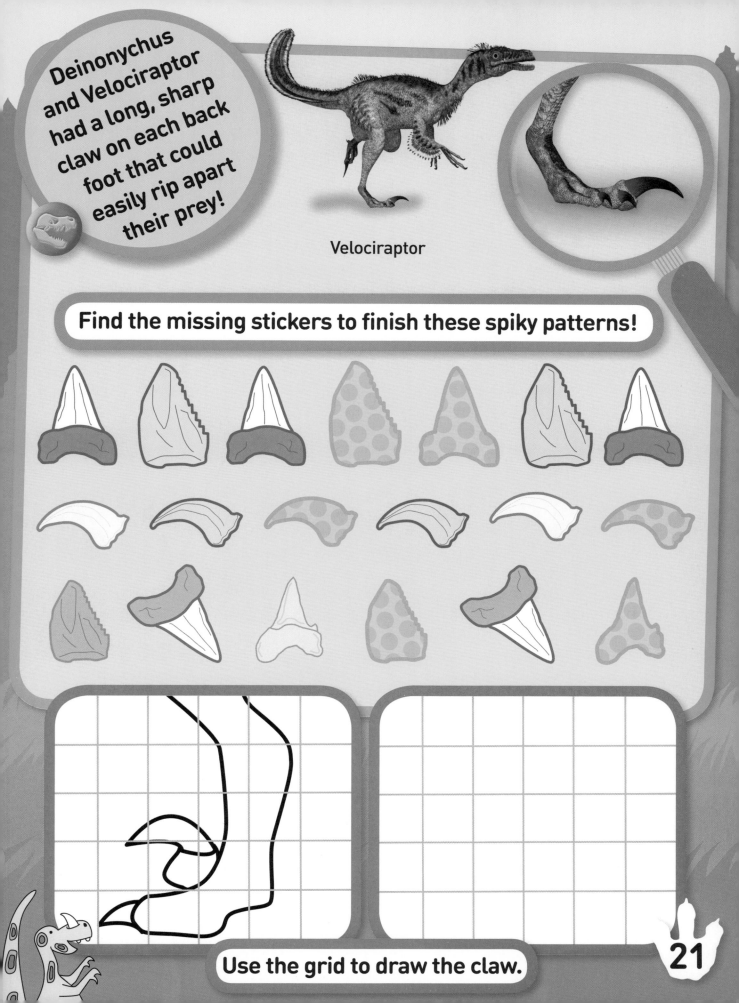

Deinonychus and Velociraptor had a long, sharp claw on each back foot that could easily rip apart their prey!

Velociraptor

Find the missing stickers to finish these spiky patterns!

Use the grid to draw the claw.

21

Herbivores were plant-eating dinos!

Connect the dots to find Ankylosaurus, then add color.

Ankylosaurus had to eat a huge amount of plants to feed itself—and probably produced a lot of gas as a result!

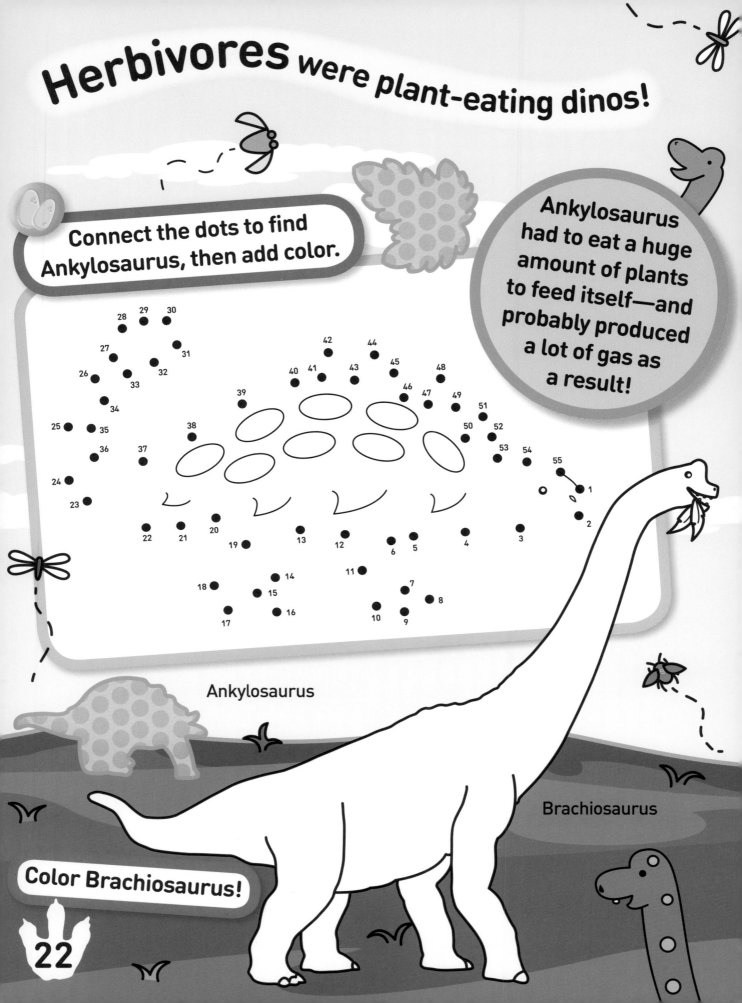

Ankylosaurus

Brachiosaurus

Color Brachiosaurus!

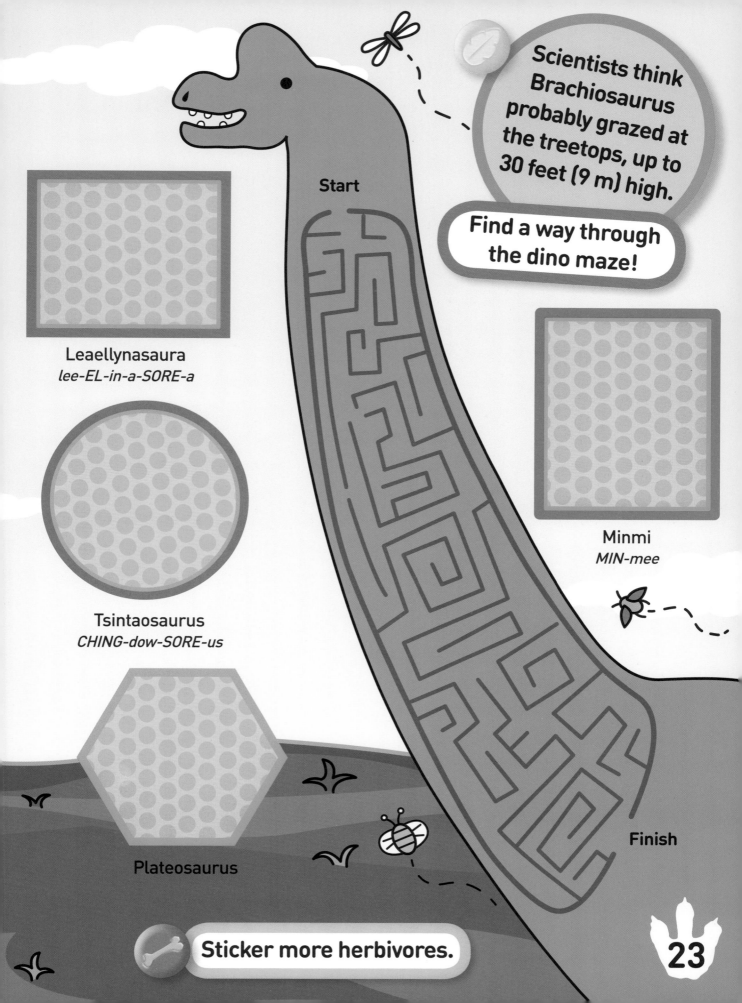

Start

Scientists think Brachiosaurus probably grazed at the treetops, up to 30 feet (9 m) high.

Find a way through the dino maze!

Leaellynasaura
lee-EL-in-a-SORE-a

Tsintaosaurus
CHING-dow-SORE-us

Plateosaurus

Minmi
MIN-mee

Finish

Sticker more herbivores.

23

Triceratops means three-horned face!

Sticker horns for Triceratops.

Triceratops's skull was huge and was one third of the length of its whole body.

Triceratops had cool features!

BEAK-LIKE MOUTH

BONY FRILL

Sticker more plants for Triceratops to eat.

Find five tiny Triceratops hiding from T. rex!

Draw, color, and sticker to complete the dinosaur dig!

T. rex

Scientists think that Triceratops was often hunted by T. rex.

Draw your own skull.

Who's hiding underground?

Connect the dots to finish the skull.

Amazing armored dinosaurs

Stegosaurus had huge bony plates and tail spikes!

Sticker and color Stegosaurus's plates.

Start

Ankylosaurus's belly was the only part of its body not covered in armor!

Finish

Help Stegosaurus reach its food without running into Allosaurus or Ceratosaurus.

With its club-tail, Ankylosaurus was ready for battle!

Find the missing stickers to armor Ankylosaurus!

Stegosaurus's brain was only about the size of a tangerine!

Use the grid to draw the dino.

Stegosaurus

Giant sauropods had **long necks!**

Sticker more leaves for these sauropod dinosaurs.

Sauropods were massive, plant-eating dinosaurs. They had enormous bodies, but their heads were tiny!

Give these dinosaurs colorful, long necks!

Sticker everyday objects to show how big these beasts were!

Mamenchisaurus
mah-MEHN-chee-SORE-us

Argentinosaurus
arh-gen-TEEN-oh-SORE-us

Mamenchisaurus and Argentinosaurus were two of the biggest dinosaurs in the world!

Diplodocus

Sticker more dinosaur footprints!

You could take a bath in one of Diplodocus's footprints!

Apatosaurus
uh-PAT-uh-SORE-us

29

Discover **duck-billed** dinos!

Sticker the duck-billed dinos and draw lines to match the pairs.

Parasaurolophus

Saurolophus
SORE-oh-LOAF-us

Lambeosaurus
LAM-bee-oh-SORE-us

Corythosaurus
co-RITH-oh-SORE-us

HONK!

Parasaurolophus may have made honking sounds using the crest on its head!

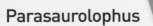

Sticker a colorful song for these noisy dinosaurs!

Corythosaurus

Edmontosaurus
ed-MON-toh-SORE-us

Draw yourself riding on a Parasaurolophus!

Humans have up to 32 teeth, but some duck-billed dinosaurs had up to 1,500!

Finish

Start

Help Mother Parasaurolophus find her three babies!

31

Fun, **feathered** dinosaurs

Make the feathers bright and colorful!

Caudipteryx
caw-DIP-turr-iks

Caudipteryx had a feathery tail and was the size of a peacock. Scientists cannot agree whether it was a dinosaur or a bird!

Find the missing stickers, then find which tail is different.

Draw the other half of the tail.

Help Caudipteryx find seeds and insects to eat!

Microraptor was another feathered dinosaur. It even had feathers on its back legs!

Microraptor

Sticker some friends for Microraptor!

33

Incredible creatures filled the oceans!

These amazing creatures lived in or near water. They were not dinosaurs.

Elasmosaurus

Plesiosaurus
plee-zee-oh-SORE-us

Finish

Start

34

Help Plesiosaurus swim through the sea without hitting any rocks or fish!

Ticinosuchus
tih-SEEN-oh-SOO-kus

Deinosuchus
die-no-SOO-kus

Ticinosuchus was a small, powerful predator that hunted the swamps for its prey.

Deinosuchus was a giant crocodile. It grew up to 36 feet (11 m) long!

Kronosaurus
KRON-oh-SORE-us

Ichthyosaurus
IK-thee-oh-SORE-us

Liopleurodon
LIE-oh-PLOO-ro-don

Color Liopleurodon!

Pterosaurs roamed the skies.

Pteranodon

After insects, pterosaurs were the next animals on Earth to fly.

Sticker and color the flying pterosaurs.

pterosaur
TER-uh-SORE

Rhamphorhynchus
RAM-foh-RING-khus

Pteranodon

Sticker more fish!

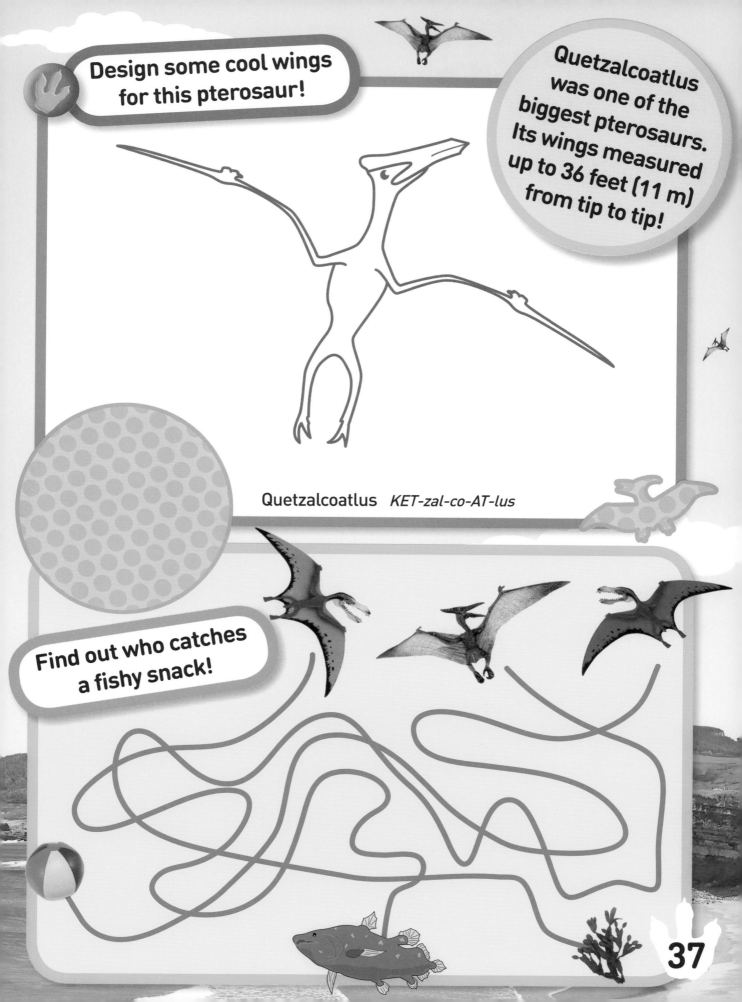

Design some cool wings for this pterosaur!

Quetzalcoatlus was one of the biggest pterosaurs. Its wings measured up to 36 feet (11 m) from tip to tip!

Quetzalcoatlus   *KET-zal-co-AT-lus*

Find out who catches a fishy snack!

Be a fossil hunter!

Connect the dots to discover the fossil!

We know about dinosaurs from the fossils of their bones and teeth, which are often found in rocks.

Use the grid to draw the fossil!

Sticker and color to finish the dino dig!

Find six hidden blue teeth fossils.

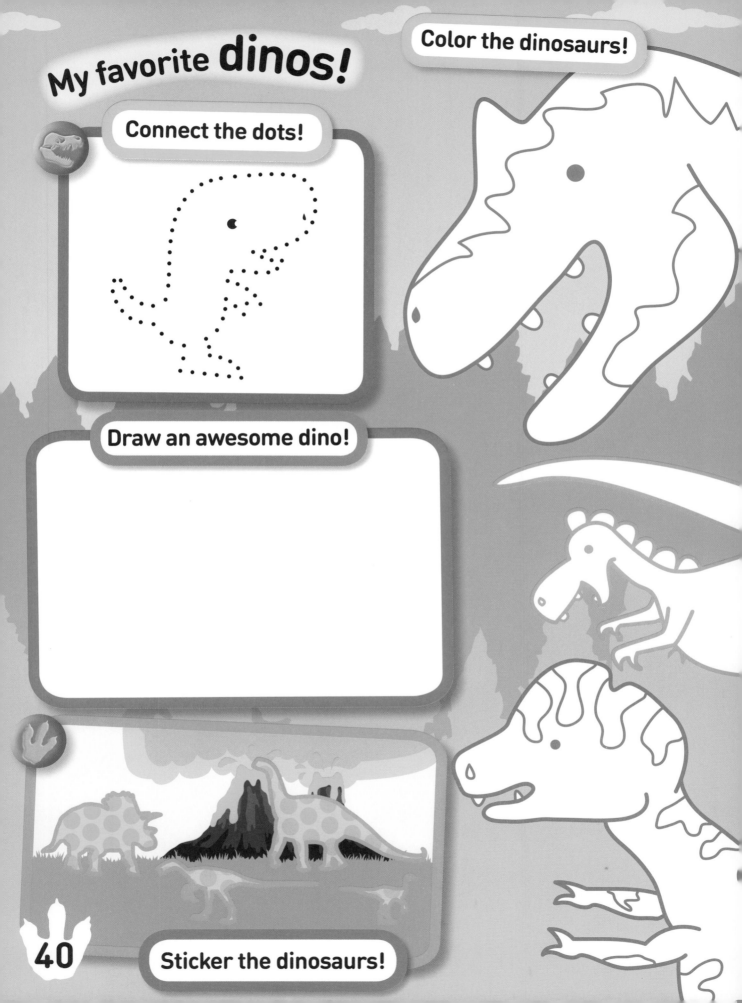

My favorite **dinos!**

Connect the dots!

Color the dinosaurs!

Draw an awesome dino!

40

Sticker the dinosaurs!

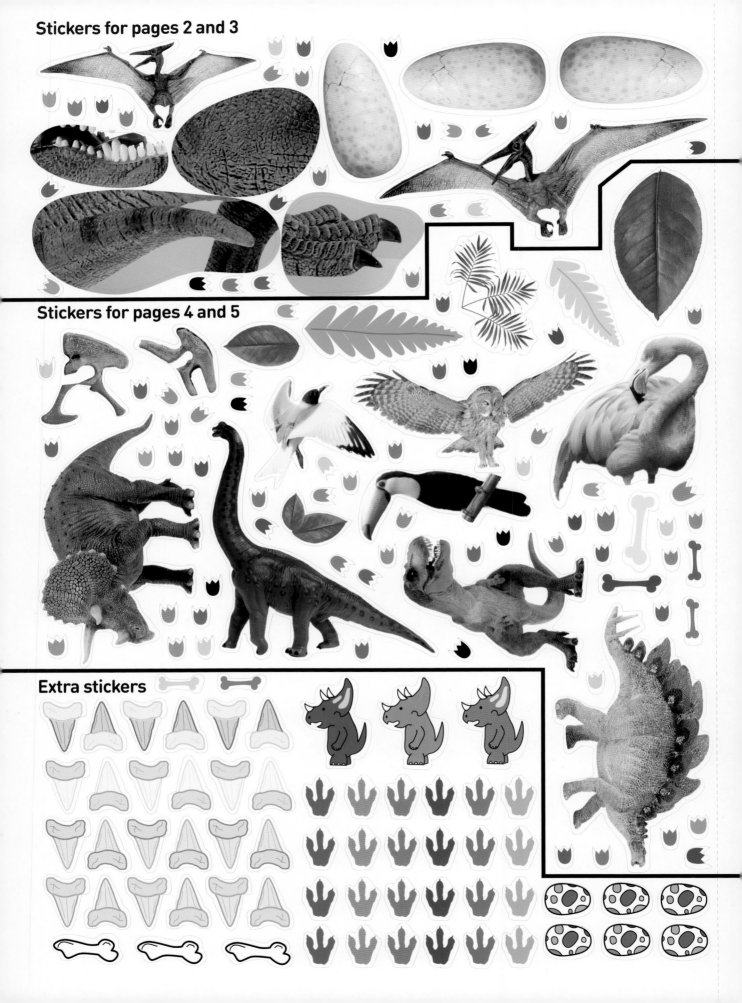

Stickers for pages 2 and 3

Stickers for pages 4 and 5

Extra stickers

Stickers for pages 6 and 7

Stickers for pages 8 and 9

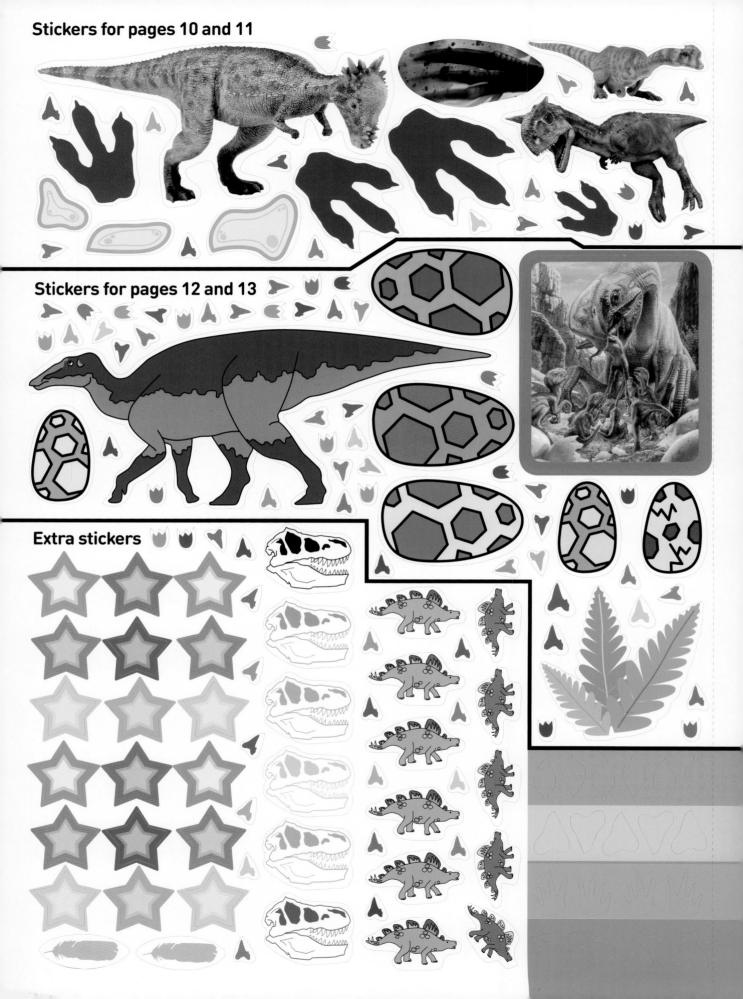

Stickers for pages 10 and 11

Stickers for pages 12 and 13

Extra stickers

Stickers for pages 14 and 15

Stickers for pages 16 and 17

Stickers for pages 18 and 19

Stickers for pages 18 and 19 continued

Stickers for pages 20 and 21

Stickers for pages 22 and 23

Stickers for pages 24 and 25

Stickers for pages 26 and 27

Stickers for pages 28 and 29

Stickers for pages 30 and 31

Extra stickers

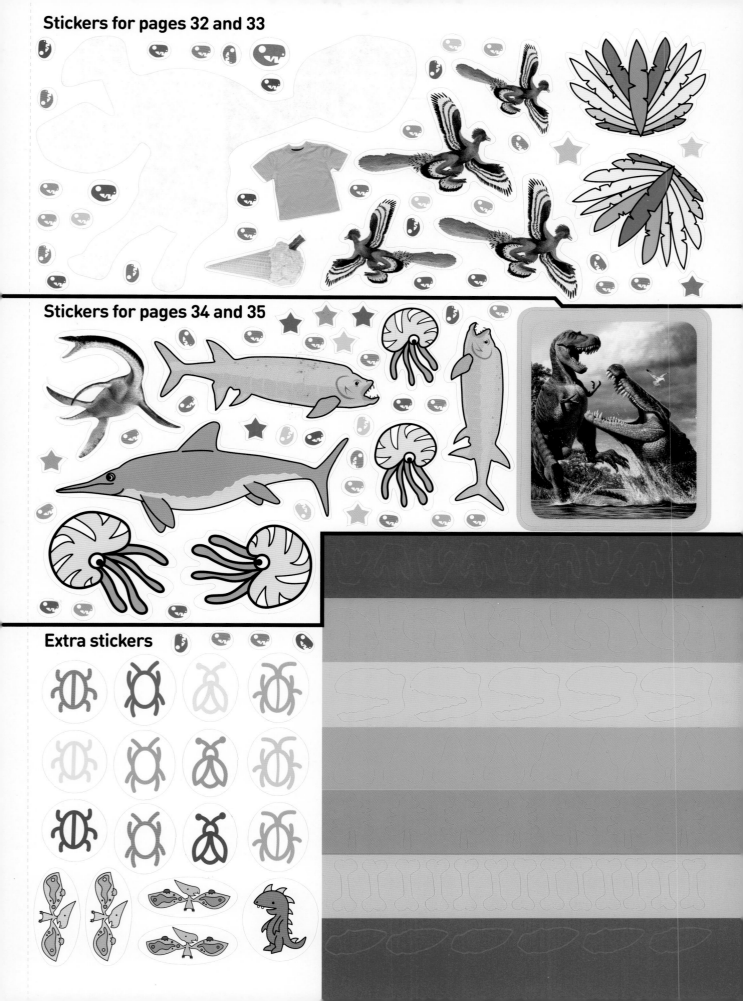

Stickers for pages 32 and 33

Stickers for pages 34 and 35

Extra stickers

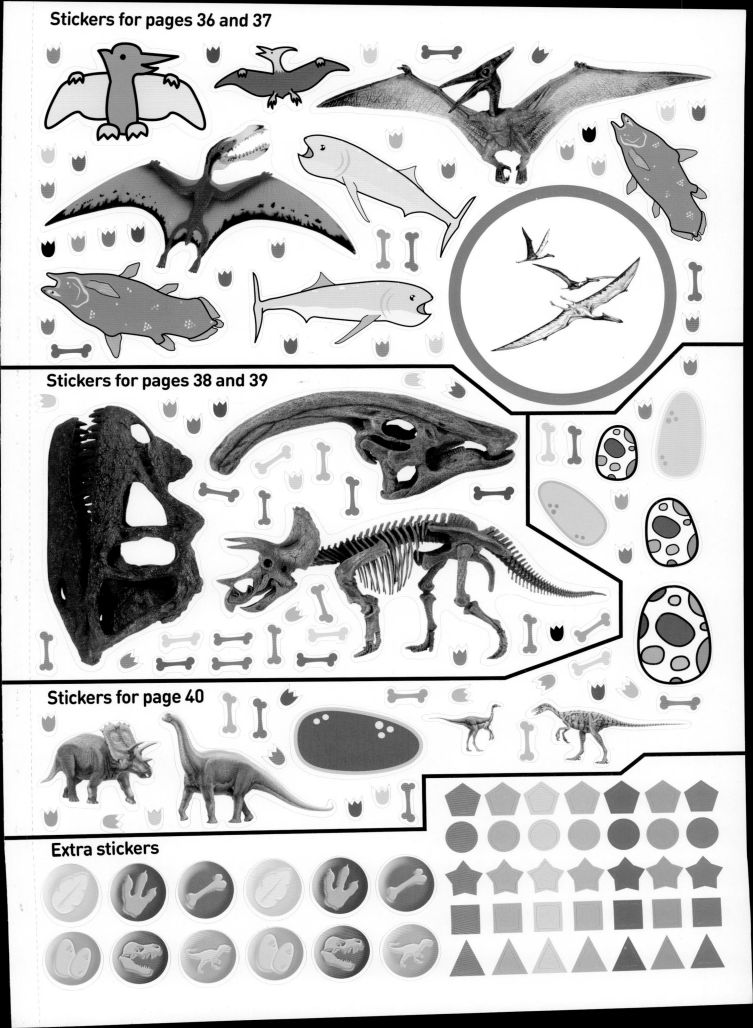

Stickers for pages 36 and 37

Stickers for pages 38 and 39

Stickers for page 40

Extra stickers